TRULY
T·O·T·A·L·L·Y
TRUMP

—— TRULY——
T·O·T·A·L·L·Y
TRUMP

A COLLECTION OF
Put-Downs, Insults &
Unforgettable Utterances
FROM A PRESIDENT
WHO TELLS IT LIKE IT IS

JOHN FORD

Castle Point Books
New York

www.stmartins.com
www.castlepointbooks.com

The Castle Point Books trademark is owned by
Castle Point Publishing, LLC.
Castle Point books are published and distributed by
St. Martin's Press.

Designed by Tara Long

ISBN 978-1-250-20154-6 (hardcover)

Our books may be purchased in bulk for promotional, educational,
or business use. Please contact your local bookseller or the
Macmillan Corporate and Premium Sales Department at
1-800-221-7945, extension 5442, or by email at
MacmillanSpecialMarkets@macmillan.com.

First Edition: September 2018

10 9 8 7 6 5 4 3 2 1

CONTENTS

DUMMIES

WOW, THE RIDICULOUS
DEAL MADE BETWEEN
LYIN'TED CRUZ AND 1
FOR 42 JOHN KASICH
HAS JUST BLOWN UP.
What a dumb deal—
dead on arrival!

TWITTER, APRIL 29, 2016

OUR PRESIDENT IS A GREAT EMBARRASSMENT TO THE U.S. HOW COULD ANYBODY BE SO DUMB OR KNOW SO LITTLE AS TO MAKE THE VERY STUPID 5 FOR I SWAP?

TWITTER, JUNE 3, 2014

Why are @JebBush flunkies @ananavarro and @secupp, **TWO OF THE DUMBEST PEOPLE IN POLITICS,** always on the @CNN panels... and yet Poll:Trump 39

TWITTER, DECEMBER 27, 2015

@EWErickson is a total low life—read his past tweets. **A DUMMY WITH NO "IT" FACTOR.** Will fade fast.

TWITTER, OCTOBER 8, 2015, ABOUT ERICK ERICKSON, CONSERVATIVE COMMENTATOR

Really dumb @CheriJacobus.

BEGGED MY PEOPLE FOR A JOB. TURNED HER DOWN TWICE AND SHE WENT HOSTILE.

Major loser, zero credibility!

TWITTER, FEBRUARY 5, 2016,
ABOUT CHERI JACOBUS, GOP CONSULTANT

@RICHLOWRY IS TRULY ONE OF THE DUMBEST OF THE TALKING HEADS—

he doesn't have a clue!

TWITTER, SEPTEMBER 21, 2015,
ABOUT RICH LOWRY, EDITOR, *NATIONAL REVIEW*

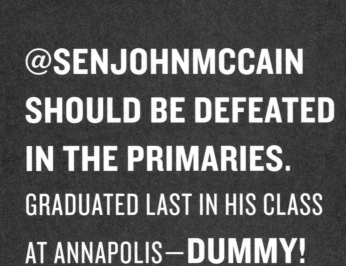

@SENJOHNMCCAIN SHOULD BE DEFEATED IN THE PRIMARIES. GRADUATED LAST IN HIS CLASS AT ANNAPOLIS—DUMMY!

TWITTER, JULY 16, 2015,
ABOUT JOHN MCCAIN, UNITED STATES SENATOR

What a waste of time being interviewed by @andersoncooper when he puts on really stupid talking heads like Tim O'Brien— **dumb guy with no clue!**

TWITTER, JULY 23, 2015,
ABOUT TIM O'BRIEN, JOURNALIST, BLOOMBERG

GREAT JOB @MARIATCARDONA ON @THISWEEKABC. YOU MADE KOOKY COKIE ROBERTS AND @BILLKRISTOL LOOK EVEN DUMBER THAN THEY ARE. **YOU WILL BE RIGHT!**

TWITTER, NOVEMBER 29, 2015, ABOUT COKIE ROBERTS, CONTRIBUTOR, *MORNING EDITION*

DUMMY @KARLROVE
CONTINUES TO
MAKE AND WRITE
FALSE STATEMENTS.
HE STILL THINKS
ROMNEY WON—
he should get a life!

TWITTER, DECEMBER 10, 2015, ABOUT KARL ROVE,
FORMER DEPUTY WHITE HOUSE CHIEF OF STAFF

Why does @Greta have a fired Bushy like dummy, John Sununu on-spewing false info? **I WILL BEAT HILLARY BY A LOT, SHE WANTS NO PART OF TRUMP.**

TWITTER, JANUARY 21, 2016

Weak and totally conflicted people like @TheRickWilson shouldn't be allowed on television unless given an I.Q. test. Dumb as a rock! @CNN

TWITTER, DECEMBER 9, 2015,
ABOUT RICK WILSON, POLITICAL CONSULTANT

I TRULY BELIEVE THAT *our country has the worst and dumbest negotiators* OF VIRTUALLY ANY COUNTRY IN THE WORLD.

TWITTER, NOVEMBER 28, 2013

Obama' ststement [*sic*] on Egypt was

TERRIBLE AND DUMB–

now being used by military as a rallying cry– our foreign policy is worst in U.S. history.

TWITTER, AUGUST 15, 2013

HIGHLY UNTALENTED WASH POST BLOGGER, **JENNIFER RUBIN, A REAL DUMMY,** NEVER WRITES FAIRLY ABOUT ME. WHY DOES WASH POST HAVE LOW IQ PEOPLE?

TWITTER, DECEMBER 1, 2015

Please explain to the dummies at the @WSJ Editorial Board **THAT I LOVE TO DEBATE AND HAVE WON**, according to Drudge etc., **ALL 11 OF THEM!**

TWITTER, MARCH 17, 2016

Isn't it funny that I am now #1 in the money losing @HuffingtonPost (poll), AND BY A BIG MARGIN. Dummy @ariannahuff must be thrilled!

TWITTER, JULY 25, 2015

SORRY, @ROSIE IS A MENTALLY SICK WOMAN, *a bully, a dummy and, above all, a loser.* OTHER THAN THAT SHE IS JUST WONDERFUL!

TWITTER, DECEMBER 8, 2014,
ABOUT ROSIE O'DONNELL, COMEDIAN

THE POLLS HAVE BEEN REALLY
AMAZING—WE ARE ALL TIRED OF
INCOMPETENT POLITICIANS AND BAD DEALS!

TWITTER, AUGUST 17, 2015

N★A★S★T★Y WOMEN

DID CROOKED HILLARY

help disgusting (check
out sex tape and past)
Alicia M become a
U.S. citizen so she could
use her in the debate?

TWITTER, SEPTEMBER 30, 2016,
ABOUT ALICIA MACHADO, FORMER MISS UNIVERSE

I GAVE A WOMAN NAMED BARBARA RES A TOP N.Y. CONSTRUCTION JOB,

when that was unheard of, and now she is nasty. **SO MUCH FOR A NICE THANK YOU!**

TWITTER, MAY 16, 2016, ABOUT BARBARA RES, FORMER TRUMP EXECUTIVE AND AUTHOR OF *ALL ALONE ON THE 68TH FLOOR: HOW ONE WOMAN CHANGED THE FACE OF CONSTRUCTION*

@JRubinBlogger one of the dumber bloggers @washingtonpost only writes purposely inaccurate pieces on me. *She is in love with Marco Rubio?*

TWITTER, DECEMBER 4, 2015

Justice Ginsburg of the U.S. Supreme Court **HAS EMBARRASSED ALL BY MAKING VERY DUMB POLITICAL STATEMENTS ABOUT ME.** Her mind is shot—resign!

TWITTER, JULY 12, 2016

THE ARROGANT
YOUNG WOMAN WHO
QUESTIONED ME IN
SUCH A NASTY
FASHION AT NO
LABELS YESTERDAY
**WAS A JEB STAFFER!
HOW CAN HE BEAT
RUSSIA & CHINA?**

TWITTER, OCTOBER 13, 2015

Hillary just said that she will not use the term **"RADICAL ISLAMIC"** – but was incapable of saying why. She is afraid of Obama & the e-mails!

TWITTER, DECEMBER 6, 2015

Lightweight Senator Kirsten Gillibrand, **A TOTAL FLUNKY FOR CHUCK SCHUMER** and someone who would come to my office "begging" for campaign contributions not so long ago (and would do anything for them), is now in the ring fighting against Trump. **VERY DISLOYAL TO BILL & CROOKED—USED!**

TWITTER, DECEMBER 12, 2017,

KATIE COURIC, THE THIRD RATE REPORTER, WHO HAS BEEN LARGELY FORGOTTEN, should be ashamed of herself for the fraudulent editing of her doc.

TWITTER, MAY 31, 2016

KATHY GRIFFIN SHOULD BE ASHAMED OF HERSELF. My children, especially my 11 year old son, Barron, are having a hard time with this. SICK!

TWITTER, MAY 31, 2017,
ABOUT KATHY GRIFFIN, COMEDIAN, ACTRESS

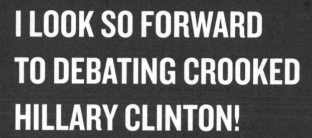

I LOOK SO FORWARD TO DEBATING CROOKED HILLARY CLINTON!

Democrat Primaries are rigged, e-mail investigation is rigged -

SO TIME TO GET IT ON!

TWITTER, MAY 17, 2016,
ABOUT INVESTIGATION OF HILLARY CLINTON'S E-MAIL

Ungrateful traitor Chelsea Manning, who should never have been released from prison, is now calling *President Obama a weak leader.* Terrible!

TWITTER, JANUARY 26, 2017, ABOUT CHELSEA MANNING, WHISTLEBLOWER, FORMER SOLDIER

MISS UNIVERSE, PAULINA VEGA,

CRITICIZED ME FOR TELLING THE TRUTH ABOUT ILLEGAL IMMIGRATION, BUT THEN SAID SHE WOULD KEEP THE CROWN—

HYPOCRITE

TWITTER, JULY 5, 2015,
ABOUT PAULINA VEGA, FORMER MISS UNIVERSE

POCAHONTAS IS AT IT AGAIN!

Goofy Elizabeth Warren, one of the least productive U.S. Senators, has a nasty mouth. **Hope she is V.P. choice.**

TWITTER, JUNE 10, 2016,
ABOUT ELIZABETH WARREN, UNITED STATES SENATOR

Huma Abedin, the top aide to Hillary Clinton and the wife of **PERV SLEAZEBAG ANTHONY WIENER,** was a major security risk as a collector of info

TWITTER, AUGUST 31, 2015, ABOUT HUMA ABEDIN, VICE CHAIR OF THE 2016 HILLARY CLINTON PRESIDENTIAL CAMPAIGN

HILLARY SAID SUCH NASTY THINGS ABOUT ME, read directly off her teleprompter . . . but there was no emotion, no truth. **JUST CAN'T READ SPEECHES!**

TWITTER, SEPTEMBER 5, 2015

If it were up to goofy Elizabeth Warren, we'd have no jobs in America—*she doesn't have a clue.*

TWITTER, MAY 11, 2016

@MEGYNKELLY IS VERY BAD AT MATH. SHE WAS TOTALLY UNABLE TO FIGURE OUT THE DIFFERENCE BETWEEN ME AND CRUZ IN THE NEW MONMOUTH POLL **41TO14.**

TWITTER, DECEMBER 15, 2015

I feel sorry for Rosie's new partner in love whose parents are devastated at the thought of their daughter being with @Rosie—

A TRUE LOSER.

TWITTER, DECEMBER 14, 2011

I LOVE WOMEN. They've come into my life. **THEY'VE GONE OUT OF MY LIFE.** Even those who have exited somewhat ungracefully still have a place in my heart. **I ONLY HAVE ONE REGRET IN THE WOMEN DEPARTMENT**—that I never had the opportunity to court Lady Diana Spencer.

TRUMP: THE ART OF THE COMEBACK (1997)

THE
ENEMY
OF THE
PEOPLE

So much Fake News being put in dying magazines and newspapers. Only place worse may be @NBCNews, @CBSNews, @ABC and @CNN.

FICTION WRITERS!

TWITTER, OCTOBER 17, 2017

MANY JOURNALISTS
ARE HONEST AND
GREAT—BUT SOME ARE
KNOWINGLY DISHONEST
AND BASIC SCUM.
**THEY SHOULD.BE
WEEDED OUT!**

TWITTER, APRIL 6, 2015

Just watched the *totally biased and fake news reports* of the so-called Russia story on NBC and ABC. **Such dishonesty!**

TWITTER, MARCH 23, 2017

ACCORDING TO THE @NYTIMES, A RUSSIAN SOLD PHONY SECRETS ON "TRUMP" TO THE U.S.

Asking price was $10 million, brought down to $1 million to be paid over time. I hope people are now seeing & understanding what is going on here. It is all now starting to come out —

DRAIN THE SWAMP!

TWITTER, FEBRUARY 10, 2018

I HEARD POORLY RATED @MORNING_JOE SPEAKS BADLY OF ME (DON'T WATCH ANYMORE). THEN HOW COME LOW I.Q. CRAZY MIKA, ALONG WITH PSYCHO JOE, CAME TO MAR-A-LAGO 3 NIGHTS IN A ROW AROUND NEW YEAR'S EVE, AND INSISTED ON JOINING ME. SHE WAS BLEEDING BADLY FROM A FACE-LIFT. **I SAID NO!**

TWITTER, JUNE 29, 2017,
ABOUT JOE SCARBOROUGH AND MIKA BRZEZINSKI,
HOSTS, *MORNING JOE*

Even Crazy Jim Acosta of Fake News CNN agrees: **"Trump World and WH sources dancing in end zone:** Trump wins again . . . Schumer and Dems caved . . . gambled and lost." **Thank you for your honesty Jim!**

TWITTER, JANUARY 23, 2018

IF @AMAZON EVER HAD TO PAY FAIR TAXES, ITS STOCK WOULD CRASH AND IT WOULD CRUMBLE LIKE A PAPER BAG. THE @WASHINGTONPOST SCAM IS SAVING IT!

TWITTER, DECEMBER 7, 2015

MICHAEL BARBARO,

THE AUTHOR OF THE NOW
DISCREDITED @NYTIMES HIT PIECE
ON ME WITH WOMEN, HAS IN PAST
TWEETED BADLY ABOUT ME.
HE SHOULD RESIGN

TWITTER, MAY 17, 2016

Some low-life journalist claims that I "made a pass" at her 29 years ago. **NEVER HAPPENED!** Like the @nytimes story which has become a joke!

TWITTER, MAY 18, 2016

Wow, @CNN is really working hard to make me look as bad as possible. **Very unprofessional. Hurting in ratings—** ***bad television!***

TWITTER, MAY 14, 2016

NEW DAY ON CNN TREATS ME VERY BADLY.

@AlisynCamerota is a disaster.

NOT GOING TO WATCH ANYMORE.

TWITTER, JANUARY 21, 2016

ESPN is paying
a really big price
for its politics (and
bad programming).
People are
dumping it in
RECORD numbers.
**APOLOGIZE
FOR UNTRUTH!**

TWITTER, SEPTEMBER 15, 2017

SMALL CROWDS AT @REDSTATE TODAY IN ATLANTA. PEOPLE WERE VERY ANGRY AT EWERICKSON, **a major sleaze and buffoon** WHO HAS SAVED ME TIME AND MONEY

TWITTER, AUGUST 8, 2015

@MajorCBS
Major Garrett of
@CBSNews covers
me very inaccurately.
*Total agenda,
bad reporter!*

TWITTER, JANUARY 11, 2016, ABOUT MAJOR GARRETT,
WHITE HOUSE CORRESPONDENT, CBS NEWS

THE RATINGS
FOR THE VIEW
ARE REALLY LOW.
NICOLE WALLACE AND
MOLLY SIMS ARE A DISASTER.
GET NEW CAST OR JUST PUT IT
TO SLEEP. DEAD T.V.

TWITTER, JUNE 24, 2015,
ABOUT HOSTS OF *THE VIEW*

A big fat hit job on
@oreillyfactor tonight.
**A total waste of time to
watch, boring and biased.**
@brithume said I would
never run, **A DOPE!**

TWITTER, FEBRUARY 22, 2016,
ABOUT BRIT HUME, POLITICAL ANALYST, FOX NEWS

I HEAR THAT SLEEPY EYES @CHUCKTODD WILL BE FIRED LIKE A DOG FROM RATINGS STARVED MEET THE PRESS? I CAN'T IMAGINE WHAT IS TAKING SO LONG!

TWITTER, JULY 12, 2015,
ABOUT CHUCK TODD

With all of its phony unnamed sources & highly slanted & even fraudulent reporting, #**Fake News is DISTORTING DEMOCRACY** in our country!

TWITTER, JULY 16, 2017

Watched Saturday Night Live hit job on me. **Time to retire the boring and unfunny show.** Alec Baldwin portrayal stinks. *Media rigging election!*

TWITTER, OCTOBER 16, 2016

DOPES

@AC360 HAS THE ABSOLUTELY WORST ANTI-TRUMP TALKING HEADS ON HIS SHOW. DOPEY WRITER O'BRIAN KNOWS NOTHING ABOUT ME OR MY WEALTH. **A WASTE!**

TWITTER, JULY 22, 2015,
ABOUT AUTHOR TIM O'BRIEN

You mean George Bush sends our soldiers into combat, they are severely wounded, **AND THEN HE WANTS $120,000 TO MAKE A BORING SPEECH TO THEM?**

TWITTER, JULY 9, 2015

Jeb's big ad buy against me, paid for by lobbyists, shows my face but doesn't have me answering Jeb's statements. *He is really pathetic!*

TWITTER, DECEMBER 22, 2015

The Al Frankenstien [*sic*] picture is really bad, speaks a thousand words.

WHERE DO HIS HANDS GO IN PICTURES 2, 3, 4, 5 & 6 WHILE SHE SLEEPS? . . . . .

TWITTER, NOVEMBER 16, 2017

Never met but never liked dopey Robert Gates.

LOOK AT THE MESS THE U.S. IS IN.

Always speaks badly of his many bosses, including Obama.

TWITTER, SEPTEMBER 17, 2016, ABOUT ROBERT GATES,
FORMER SECRETARY OF DEFENSE

Woody Johnson, owner of the NYJets, is @JebBush's finance chairman.

IF WOODY WOULD'VE BEEN W/ ME, HE WOULD'VE BEEN IN THE PLAYOFFS, AT LEAST!

TWITTER, JANUARY 4, 2016, ABOUT WOODY JOHNSON, OWNER, NEW YORK JETS

JUST HEARD FOREIGN MINISTER
OF NORTH KOREA SPEAK AT U.N.
**If he echoes thoughts
of Little Rocket Man,
they won't be around
much longer!**

TWITTER, SEPTEMBER 23, 2017,
ABOUT KIM JONG-UN, LEADER OF NORTH KOREA

. . . our Great American Flag (or Country) and should stand for the National Anthem. If not, **YOU'RE FIRED.** *Find something else to do!*

TWITTER, SEPTEMBER 23, 2017,
ABOUT COLIN KAEPERNICK, PROFESSIONAL FOOTBALL PLAYER

DOPEY @LAWRENCE O'DONNELL, **WHOSE UNWATCHABLE SHOW IS DYING IN THE RATINGS,** SAID THAT MY APPRENTICE$ NUMBERS WERE WRONG. **HE IS A FOOL!**

TWITTER, JULY 16, 2015,
ABOUT *THE LAST WORD WITH LAWRENCE O'DONNELL*

@GOVERNORPATAKI couldn't be elected dog catcher if he ran again— SO HE DIDN'T!

TWITTER, JULY 1, 2015, ABOUT GEORGE PATAKI, FORMER NEW YORK GOVERNOR

Tom Ridge should be focused on trying to bring the party together rather than ripping it apart w/ your faulty thought process.

I WILL WIN!

TWITTER, DECEMBER 11, 2015, ABOUT TOM RIDGE,
FORMER PENNSYLVANIA GOVERNOR

Dopey Prince @Alwaleed_Talal **wants to control our U.S. politicians with daddy's money.** Can't do it when I get elected. **#Trump2016**

TWITTER, DECEMBER 11, 2015,
ABOUT PRINCE ALWALEED BIN TALAL, OF SAUDI ARABIA

@BOBVANDERPLAATS IS A TOTAL PHONY AND DISHONEST GUY. ASKED ME FOR EXPENSIVE HOTEL ROOMS, FREE (AND MORE). I SAID PAY AND HE ENDORSED CRUZ!

TWITTER, JANUARY 31, 2016, ABOUT BOB VANDER PLAATS, PRESIDENT AND CHIEF EXECUTIVE, THE FAMILY LEADER

I SKIPPED A SPEECH
GIVEN YEARS AGO AT
MAR-A-LAGO BY
DOPEY @GEORGEWILL
BECAUSE HE'S BORING—
he never forgot!

TWITTER, NOVEMBER 19, 2015,
ABOUT GEORGE WILL, COLUMNIST

North Korean Leader Kim Jong Un just stated that the "Nuclear Button is on his desk at all times." Will someone from his depleted and food starved regime **please inform him that I too have a Nuclear Button, but it is a much bigger & more powerful one than his, AND MY BUTTON WORKS!**

TWITTER, JANUARY 2, 2018

THE
DEMS

Heading to beautiful West Virginia to be with great members of the Republican Party. Will be planning Infrastructure and discussing Immigration and DACA, not easy when we have no support from the Democrats.

NOT ONE DEM VOTED FOR OUR TAX CUT BILL! Need more Republicans in '18.

TWITTER, FEBRUARY 1, 2018

I would rather run against **Crooked Hillary Clinton than Bernie Sanders** AND THAT WILL HAPPEN BECAUSE THE BOOKS ARE COOKED AGAINST BERNIE!

TWITTER, MAY 4, 2016

With Democrats **SPITZER, DANGER-WEINER & FILNER,** which party really has the war on women?

TWITTER, AUGUST 21, 2013

Exxon donated $250g
to Obama's inaugural
http://bit.ly/XzHytP
*I guess the
Democrats have
no problem
accepting money
from 'big oil.'*

TWITTER, JANUARY 23, 2013

SLEAZY ADAM SCHIFF, THE TOTALLY BIASED CONGRESSMAN LOOKING INTO "RUSSIA," spends all of his time on television pushing the Dem loss excuse!

TWITTER, JULY 24, 2017,
ABOUT ADAM SCHIFF, UNITED STATES CONGRESSMAN

@BARACKOBAMA HARD AT WORK YESTERDAY SHOOTING A MARSHMALLOW CANNON IN THE WH EAST ROOM WHILE OUR COUNTRY BURNS. HTTP://BIT.LY/WICXJD

TWITTER, FEBRUARY 8, 2012

If Cory Booker is the future of the Democratic Party, **they have no future!** I know more about Cory than he knows about himself.

TWITTER, JULY 25, 2016,
ABOUT CORY BOOKER, UNITED STATES SENATOR

I was viciously attacked by Mr. Khan at the Democratic Convention. Am I not allowed to respond? **HILLARY VOTED FOR THE IRAQ WAR, NOT ME!**

TWITTER, JULY 31, 2016,
ABOUT KHIZR KHAN, FATHER OF FALLEN
GOLD STAR U.S. ARMY CAPTAIN HUMAYUN KHAN

SOMEBODY PLEASE INFORM JAY-Z THAT BECAUSE OF MY POLICIES, **BLACK UNEMPLOYMENT HAS JUST BEEN REPORTED TO BE AT THE LOWEST RATE** EVER RECORDED!

TWITTER, JANUARY 28, 2018

The top Leadership and Investigators of the FBI and the Justice Department have politicized the sacred investigative process in favor of Democrats and against Republicans—something which would have been unthinkable just a short time ago.

RANK & FILE ARE GREAT PEOPLE!

TWITTER, FEBRUARY 2, 2018, ABOUT FBI

Little Adam Schiff, who is desperate to run for higher office, *is one of the biggest liars and leakers in Washington,* right up there with Comey, Warner, Brennan and Clapper! Adam leaves closed committee hearings to illegally leak confidential information. *Must be stopped!*

TWITTER, FEBRUARY 5, 2018

OUR GREAT AFRICAN AMERICAN
PRESIDENT HASN'T EXACTLY HAD
A POSITIVE IMPACT ON THE
**THUGS WHO ARE SO
HAPPILY AND OPENLY
DESTROYING BALTIMORE!**

TWITTER, APRIL 27, 2015

The Democrats sent a very political and long response memo which they knew, because of sources and methods (and more), would have to be heavily redacted, whcreupon they would blame the White House for lack of transparency. *Told them to re-do and send back in proper form!*

TWITTER, FEBRUARY 10, 2018

I do not understand how so many of my Jewish friends backed Obama in the last election.

HE IS A TOTAL DISASTER FOR ISRAEL—AND ALWAYS WILL BE

TWITTER, NOVEMBER 24, 2013

OUR COUNTRY NEEDS
A PRESIDENT WITH
GREAT LEADERSHIP
SKILLS AND VISION,
*not someone like
Hillary or Barack,
neither of which
has a clue!*

TWITTER, SEPTEMBER 6, 2015

I JUST HAD TO FIRE SOMEONE,
HE DIDN'T HAVE A CLUE—
HE REMINDED ME OF OBAMA
ON WEDNESDAY NIGHT.

TWITTER, OCTOBER 10, 2012

Our relationship with Russia is at an all-time & very dangerous low.

YOU CAN THANK CONGRESS, the same

people that can't even give us HCare!

TWITTER, AUGUST 3, 2017

Republicans want to fix DACA far more than the Democrats do. The Dems had all three branches of government back in 2008–2011, and they decided not to do anything about DACA. They only want to use it as a campaign issue. *Vote Republican!*

TWITTER, FEBRUARY 10, 2018

So disgraceful that a person illegally in our country killed @Colts linebacker Edwin Jackson. This is just one of many such preventable tragedies. **WE MUST GET THE DEMS TO GET TOUGH ON THE BORDER,** and with illegal immigration, FAST!

TWITTER, FEBRUARY 6, 2018

WOW, JUST IN— ObamaCare projected to cause large scale drop in jobs—even Dems are shocked by 2.5 million number.

DISASTER!

TWITTER, FEBRUARY 5, 2014

"MR. PRESIDENT, *take your campaign of division and anger and hate* BACK TO CHICAGO."
—@MITTROMNEY

TWITTER, AUGUST 16, 2012

FAILING

The United Kingdom is trying hard to disguise their massive Muslim problem. **Everybody is wise to what is happening, very sad!** *Be honest.*

TWITTER, DECEMBER 10, 2015

ENOUGH IS ENOUGH— NO MORE BUSHES!

https://instagram.com/p/6NbVyEmhdB/

TWITTER, AUGUST 10, 2015

WE MUST STOP THE CRIME AND KILLING MACHINE THAT IS ILLEGAL IMMIGRATION. RAMPANT PROBLEMS WILL ONLY GET WORSE. **TAKE BACK OUR COUNTRY!**

TWITTER, AUGUST 10, 2015

Don't like @SamuelLJackson's golf swing. **NOT ATHLETIC.** I've won many club championships. **PLAY HIM FOR CHARITY!**

TWITTER, JANUARY 6, 2016,
ABOUT SAMUEL JACKSON

PATHETIC EXCUSE
BY LONDON MAYOR
SADIQ KHAN WHO HAD
TO THINK FAST ON
HIS *"no reason to be
alarmed"* STATEMENT.
MSM IS WORKING
HARD TO SELL IT!

TWITTER, JUNE 5, 2017,
ABOUT SADIQ KHAN, MAYOR OF LONDON

@JohnLegere @TMobile John,

FOCUS ON RUNNING YOUR COMPANY,

I think the service is terrible!

Try hiring some good managers.

TWITTER, NOVEMBER 15, 2015,
ABOUT JOHN LEGERE, CHIEF EXECUTIVE, T-MOBILE

THE MAYOR OF
SAN JOSE DID A
TERRIBLE JOB OF
ORDERING THE
PROTECTION OF
INNOCENT PEOPLE.
**The thugs were
lucky supporters
remained peaceful!**

TWITTER, JUNE 4, 2016, ABOUT SAM LICCARDO,
MAYOR OF SAN JOSE, CALIFORNIA

@drmoore Russell Moore is truly a terrible representative of Evangelicals and all of the good they stand for. **A NASTY GUY WITH NO HEART!**

TWITTER, MAY 9, 2016
ABOUT RUSSELL MOORE, EVANGELICAL LEADER

Michael Morell, THE LIGHTWEIGHT FORMER ACTING DIRECTOR OF C.I.A., AND A MAN WHO HAS MADE SERIOUS BAD CALLS, *is a total Clinton flunky!*

TWITTER, AUGUST 7, 2016, ABOUT MICHAEL J. MORELL, FORMER DEPUTY DIRECTOR OF THE C.I.A.

Obama won't send troops to fight jihadists, yet sends them to Liberia to contract Ebola. **HE IS A DELUSIONAL FAILURE.**

TWITTER, OCTOBER 9, 2014

OUR VERY WEAK AND INEFFECTIVE LEADER, PAUL RYAN, had a bad conference call where his members went wild at his disloyalty.

TWITTER, OCTOBER 11, 2016,
ABOUT PAUL D. RYAN, HOUSE SPEAKER

@BenSasse looks more like a gym rat than a U.S. Senator.

How the hell did he ever get elected? @greta

TWITTER, JANUARY 29, 2016,
ABOUT BEN SASSE, UNITED STATES SENATOR

CAN YOU IMAGINE WHAT
THE OUTCRY WOULD BE IF
@SNOOPDOGG, FAILING
CAREER AND ALL, HAD AIMED
AND FIRED THE GUN AT
PRESIDENT OBAMA?
JAIL TIME!

TWITTER, MARCH 15, 2017,
ABOUT SNOOP DOGG, RAPPER

@MARCTHIESSEN IS A FAILED BUSH SPEECHWRITER WHOSE WORK WAS SO BAD THAT HE HAS NEVER BEEN ABLE TO MAKE A COMEBACK. A THIRD RATE TALENT!

TWITTER, OCTOBER 15, 2015, ABOUT MARC THIESSEN,
COLUMNIST AND FOX NEWS CONTRIBUTOR

Jeb failed as Jeb!

He gave up and enlisted
Mommy and his brother
(who got us into the quicksand
of Iraq). Spent $120 million.

Weak—no chance!

TWITTER, FEBRUARY 11, 2016, ABOUT JEB BUSH

NORTH KOREA IS A COUNTRY RULED BY A CULT.

At the center of this military cult is a deranged belief in the ruler's destiny to rule as a parent protector over a conquered Korean Peninsula.

SPEECH IN SOUTH KOREA, NOVEMBER 8, 2017, ON NORTH KOREA

GOLF MATCH? I'VE WON 18 CLUB CHAMPIONSHIPS INCLUDING THIS WEEKEND. **@MCUBAN SWINGS LIKE A LITTLE GIRL** WITH NO POWER OR TALENT. MARK'S A LOSER

TWITTER, MARCH 19, 2013 ABOUT MARK CUBAN, AMERICAN BUSINESSMAN AND INVESTOR

AS I HAVE LONG BEEN SAYING,

SOUTH AFRICA

IS A TOTAL—AND VERY

DANGEROUS—MESS.

TWITTER, APRIL 20, 2015

MITT ROMNEY

is a mixed up man who doesn't have a clue. *No wonder he lost!*

TWITTER, MARCH 18, 2016

Remember, politicians are **ALL TALK** and **NO** action. Our country is a laughing stock that is going to hell. **THE LOBBYISTS & DONORS CONTROL ALL!**

TWITTER, MAY 12, 2015

Remember this, THE WORST DOCTORS (BY FAR) ARE CELEBRITY DOCTORS. IF YOU SEE THEIR NAMES, OR READ ABOUT THEM IN THE NEWSPAPERS, ***stay away!***

TWITTER, AUGUST 31, 2014

OUR COUNTRY IS IN SERIOUS TROUBLE. We don't have victories anymore. We used to have victories, but we don't have them. When was the last time anybody saw us beating, let's say, China in a trade deal? They kill us. **I BEAT CHINA ALL THE TIME. ALL THE TIME.**

JUNE 16, 2015, CANDIDACY ANNOUNCEMENT SPEECH

[Overseas] we build a school, we build a road, they blow up the school, we build another school, we build another road, they blow them up, we build again. **IN THE MEANTIME WE CAN'T GET A FUCKING SCHOOL IN BROOKLYN.**

SPEECH IN LAS VEGAS, APRIL 28, 2011

I think the big problem this country has is being politically correct. I've been challenged by so many people and **I don't frankly have time for total political correctness.**

COMMENT IN RESPONSE TO MEGYN KELLY OF FOX NEWS AT REPUBLICAN PRIMARY DEBATE AUGUST 6, 2015

Why are we having all these people from

S--THOLE COUNTRIES

come here?

REMARK MADE DURING PRIVATE MEETING WITH LAWMAKERS, JANUARY 11, 2018, VIA THE WASHINGTON POST

Iran is playing with fire–they don't appreciate how "kind" President Obama was to them. *Not me!*

TWITTER, FEBRUARY 3, 2017

JOHN KASICH WAS MANAGING DIRECTOR OF LEHMAN BROTHERS WHEN IT CRASHED, **BRINGING DOWN THE WORLD AND RUINING PEOPLE'S LIVES. A TOTAL FAILURE!**

TWITTER, NOVEMBER 19, 2015

I hope the boycott of @Macys continues forever. So many people are cutting up their cards.

MACY'S STORES SUCK AND THEY ARE BAD FOR U.S.A.

TWITTER, JULY 16, 2015

The Mexican government forces many bad people into our country. Because they're smart. They're smarter than our leaders.

INTERVIEW WITH NBC, JULY 8, 2015

HATERS

Sorry losers and haters, but my I.Q. is one of the highest— *and you all know it!* Please don't feel so stupid or insecure, it's not your fault

TWITTER, MAY 8, 2013

MITT ROMNEY had his chance to beat a failed president but he **CHOKED LIKE A DOG.** Now he calls me racist— but I am least racist person there is

TWITTER, JUNE 11, 2016,
ABOUT MITT ROMNEY, FORMER MASSACHUSETTS GOVERNOR

GENERAL JOHN ALLEN, WHO I NEVER MET

BUT SPOKE AGAINST ME LAST NIGHT,

FAILED BADLY IN HIS FIGHT AGAINST ISIS.

HIS RECORD = BAD

#NEVERHILLARY

TWITTER, JULY 29, 2016

I wonder if I run for PRESIDENT, will the **HATERS AND LOSERS** vote for me knowing that I will **MAKE AMERICA GREAT AGAIN?** I say they will!

TWITTER, SEPTEMBER 26, 2014

I win a state in votes and then get non-representative delegates because they are offered all sorts of goodies by Cruz campaign. **BAD SYSTEM!**

TWITTER, APRIL 10, 2016

I KNOW THE **"*Governors*"** AND ***Jeb Bush,*** WHO HAS GONE NASTY WITH LIES, IS BY FAR THE WEAKEST OF THE LOT. HIS FAMILY USED PRIVATE EMINENT DOMAIN!

TWITTER, FEBRUARY 9, 2016

Working on major Trade Deal with the United Kingdom. Could be very big & exciting. **JOBS!** The E.U. is very protectionist with the U.S. STOP!

TWITTER, JULY 25, 2017

I WAS SADDENED TO SEE HOW BAD
THE RATINGS WERE ON THE EMMYS
LAST NIGHT—THE WORST EVER.
**Smartest people
of them all are the
"DEPLORABLES."**

TWITTER, SEPTEMBER 19, 2017

FAILED PRESIDENTIAL CANDIDATE
LINDSEY GRAHAM
SHOULD RESPECT ME.
I DESTROYED HIS RUN, BROUGHT HIM
FROM 7% TO 0% WHEN HE GOT OUT.
NOW NASTY!

TWITTER, MARCH 7, 2016,
ABOUT LINDSEY GRAHAM, UNITED STATES SENATOR

I unfairly get audited
by the I.R.S. almost
every single year.
I have rich friends
who never get audited.
I WONDER WHY?

TWITTER, FEBRUARY 27, 2016

@FRANKLUNTZ IS A LOW CLASS SLOB who came to my office looking for consulting work and I had zero interest. Now he picks anti-Trump panels!

TWITTER, AUGUST 7, 2015,
ABOUT FRANK LUNTZ, POLITICAL CONSULTANT

Macy's was very
disloyal to me bc of
my strong stance on
illegal immigration.
*Their stock
has crashed!*
#BoycottMacys

TWITTER, NOVEMBER 12, 2015,
ABOUT MACY'S DEPARTMENT STORE

I told you @TIME Magazine would never pick me as person of the year despite being the

BIG FAVORITE

They picked person who is ruining Germany

TWITTER, DECEMBER 9, 2015,
ABOUT ANGELA MERKEL, CHANCELLOR OF GERMANY

"Little" Michael Bloomberg, WHO NEVER HAD THE GUTS TO RUN FOR PRESIDENT, *knows nothing about me.* HIS LAST TERM AS MAYOR WAS A DISASTER!

TWITTER, JULY 29, 2016, ABOUT MICHAEL BLOOMBERG, AMERICAN BUSINESSMAN AND POLITICIAN

Remember when I recently said that **BRUSSELS IS A "HELL HOLE" AND A MESS** and the failing @nytimes wrote a critical article. **I WAS SO RIGHT!**

TWITTER, MARCH 24, 2016

Why would Kim Jong-un insult me by calling me **"old,"** when I would NEVER call him **"short and fat?"**

Oh well, I try so hard to be his friend—and maybe someday that will happen!

TWITTER, NOVEMBER 11, 2017

**CHINA WOULDN'T PROVIDE
A RED CARPET STAIRWAY
FROM AIR FORCE ONE**
AND THEN PHILIPPINES
PRESIDENT CALLS OBAMA
"THE SON OF A WHORE."
Terrible!

TWITTER, SEPTEMBER 6, 2016,
ABOUT RODRIGO DUTERTE, PRESIDENT OF THE PHILIPPINES

I loved firing goofball atheist Penn @pennjillette on The Apprentice **HE NEVER HAD A CHANCE.** Wrote letter to me begging for forgiveness.

TWITTER, JULY 16, 2015,
ABOUT PENN JILLETTE, PERFORMER

IF YOU LOOK AT SADDAM HUSSEIN,
HE KILLED TERRORISTS.
I'm not saying he was an angel,
BUT THIS GUY KILLED TERRORISTS.

THE BIG IDEA WITH DONNY DEUTSCH, 2006

I DON'T KNOW PUTIN,

have no deals in Russia, and the haters are going crazy—**yet Obama can make a deal with Iran,** #1 in terror, *no problem!*

TWITTER, FEBRUARY 7, 2017

I WOULD LIKE TO WISH EVERYONE,

including all haters and losers (of which, sadly, there are many) a truly happy and enjoyable

MEMORIAL DAY!

TWITTER, MAY 24, 2015

I told all of the haters and losers long ago

THAT IRAQ WOULD FALL, TAKE THE OIL OR GET OUT FAST! Massive waste of lives and trillions of $'s

TWITTER, JUNE 12, 2014

LOSERS AND HATERS, *even you,* AS LOW AND DUMB AS YOU ARE, CAN LEARN FROM WATCHING APPRENTICE AND CHECKING OUT MY TWEETS—*you can still succeed!*

TWITTER, MARCH 3, 2013